Barbara Forbes

five-minute florist

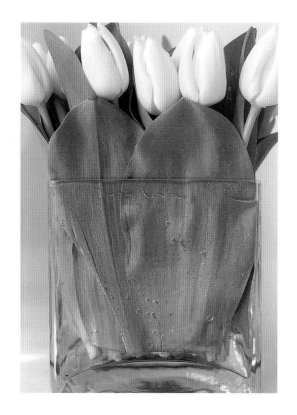

five-minute florist

bo niles

RYLAND
PETERS
& SMALL

LONDON NEW YORK

Senior designer Sally Powell
Commissioning editor Annabel Morgan
Picture researcher Emily Westlake
Production manager Patricia Harrington
Art director Gabriella Le Grazie
Publishing director Alison Starling

First published in the United Kingdom
in 2005
by Ryland Peters & Small
20–21 Jockey's Fields
London WC1R 4BW
www.rylandpeters.com

10 9 8 7 6 5 4 3 2 1

ISBN 1 84172 783 0

A CIP record for this book is available from the
British Library.

Printed and bound in China

contents

Once upon a time, the only way to acquire fresh flowers was to pick them yourself – from a meadow or roadside, or from your garden. Purchasing flowers was a luxury, and florists were few and far between. Nowadays, we are lucky – flowers are readily available from the local florist, garden centre, greengrocer or supermarket.

secret strategies for the five-minute florist

Even if you don't have time to grab a bunch of flowers on your way to the checkout, the popularity of mail order and the growth of the World Wide Web makes it possible to order and send flowers over the phone or the Internet. And you don't have to submit to seasonal dictates, for many varieties of flowers are now available all year round. Flowers are always less expensive when they are in season. But, when the mood strikes, sometimes cost is no object.

Just like cooking, arranging flowers can take time and involve intricate procedures. For those who adore working with flowers, the task poses a challenge they enjoy. For the rest of us, who have

little time but still want to enjoy flowers every day, keeping things simple, quick and easy is best.

So, what's the secret of fabulous flowers, especially if you only have a few minutes to spare? When buying flowers, pick ones that look strong and healthy, avoiding any floppy, crushed heads or drooping leaves. If you want the flowers to last for as long as possible, choose those that are not more than half-open, rather than flowers in full bloom.

Your flowers will need some basic attention before you arrange them, to guarantee that they will look their best for as long as possible. Florists call this 'conditioning', which simply means two things: number one, that you remove any leaves that will lie below the waterline in your container, to prevent bacteria from forming and hastening stem decay; and two, that you cut the stems at a 45-degree angle at the correct length for the vase. The angled cut allows water to

opposite page The most eye-catching arrangements comprise a single type of bloom in a graphic shape and colour, such as this acid-green goddess chrysanthemum bearing a feathery blast of petals. Taming stems also adds visual impact.
above left Raffia tethers flowers in a wide-mouthed vase, holding them neatly to one side, and steadying them.
above centre A pin holder anchors stems in a cylindrical vase; a bed of pebbles conceals it. For a clean look, water just covers the pebbles.
above right Stems snugly looped and bound with galvanized wire secure a bunch of narcissus for their potential container.

secret strategies

enter the stem more efficiently than if you slice it straight across (the exceptions to the rule are fleshy, hollow-stemmed flowers, such as tulips or daffodils, which can be cut straight across). When you've prepared the flowers, let them have a long drink of water before you put them in the vase they'll be displayed in. If you don't have time, don't worry, but to get the best out of your flowers you should change their water next day.

Florists know that the easiest way to create a stylish and effective arrangement is to stick with one type of flower in a single colour, so you can concentrate on the overall impact without worrying whether the blooms go together. And just as important as your choice of flower is the container in which you choose to display them. Look around your house. Virtually anything that can hold water can be used to display flowers. Even if a receptacle isn't watertight, you can insert a tumbler or jam jar inside and arrange the flowers in that. Many arrangements in this book are presented in clear glass vases, which means that the flowers are strong enough to stand on their own, using the mouth of the vase for support. Opaque containers allow you to

anchor stems with specialized steadying devices, such as floral frogs, pin holders or floral foam.

The only tools you need for the majority of simple arrangements are sharp kitchen scissors, a pair of secateurs (to cut through pithy or woody stems), and florist's wire or twine, for tying up stems. (You can use florist's tape for this purpose, too.)

Remember that most flowers have a vase life – the time they remain in water in a vase or other container in your home – of approximately five days to one week. To ensure that flowers stay healthy as long as possible, change their water every other day, adding a pinch or two of floral preservative each time.

Many people associate flowers with special occasions, such as Mother's Day, a birthday or wedding. But flowers make any day a special occasion. Pick up a bunch on your way home from work, the gym or a play date with your kids. They'll make your day.

everyday arrangements

left and above In order to give vibrant green goddess chrysanthemums full diva status, a lattice of floral sticks was constructed on top of a low, chunky vase, giving each blossom its own space in the grid. Separating blooms allows stems to dip their toes into the water, figuratively speaking, without crowding each other.

modern simplicity

above Half a dozen red tulips lie entwined in a flared bowl. Tulips hold the unique distinction of continuing to 'grow' after they are picked. As time passes, more of these will muscle their way through the water and poke their ruffled heads above its surface, perhaps spilling petals over the rim of the bowl.

Flowers, like people, come in myriad sizes and shapes. They have distinct personalities. Some are gregarious, others ingenuous. Either way, they tempt us to fall in love with them through our associations with how they look, or smell. Who can resist them?

Like people, too, flowers like to show off their plumage. To appear at their most alluring, though, they need a little help from us. The container used to show them off is important, as is the setting in which they are displayed. Traditionally, floral arrangements were proudly arrayed in the public areas of a house – the entrance hall, where flowers were proffered as a gesture of welcome; the sitting room, where floral displays were placed on dainty occasional tables; and the dining room.

But there's no reason to restrict flowers to these specific locations. Flowers are now so affordable and so easily available that we can live with them every day, all around the house – in the kitchen, the bathroom or next to the computer. Perch them on a ledge, a windowsill, the edge of the bath, the landing, or even on the floor. Be bold, too, with your container. Experiment with something that usually serves a different purpose, such as a large, glass salad bowl, or even a collection of chunky candles that have been hollowed out and stuffed with dampened floral foam to keep flower stems moist.

left Because they are almost prodigal in their ubiquity, carnations often get a bad rap. But carnations are more versatile, and varied than a clichéd buttonhole would lead you to believe. Here, a trio of pumpkin-shaped candles was carved out after their wicks burned down, then capped with sprightly red carnations, which lend them a jaunty, happy-go-lucky air.
opposite page Unlike hardy carnations, sweet peas are one of nature's most tender-stemmed flowers, and their vase life is short – just a few days. Packing them in tightly gives them strength in numbers, and shows them off in all their frothy charm.

this page and inset, right
To add panache to a bunch of white tulips, the leaves were stripped off and pressed flat against the sides of a heavy cubic vase. Once the tulips were set in position, more leaves were threaded amongst them, to provide visual and physical support. The deep green also adds a welcome counterpoint to the white-on-white room scheme.

EDWARD LUCIE-SMITH
and ELISABETH FRINK

TRAITS

left and below A harbinger of spring, grape hyacinth (or muscari) is fabulously fragrant. In a casual kitchen setting, it has been packed as tightly as possible – leaves and all – in a hurricane-style glass vase, which draws attention to the intricate structure of the bell-like blooms.

Simple, modern rooms, especially those sparsely furnished in a monochromatic palette, are particularly well-suited to an animated dialogue with their floral occupants. Against an understated backdrop, the colour, shape and texture of every blossom and stem can stand out. In such surroundings, every flower can be appreciated on its own, as well as within the context of the arrangement, especially when blossoms and leaves are exhibited in a shapely vase or container. Neutral backgrounds provide the perfect foil for flowers in vibrant colours. And white-on-white never goes out of style, especially when offset by foliage.

The key to arranging flowers in a simple, modern fashion is never to lose sight of the first word of that phrase: 'simple'. A simple container, be it clear or

Neutral backgrounds provide a perfect foil for flowers in vibrant colours.

left 'Look, no hands!' Striking blossoms are fun to experiment with. Here, gerbera daisies shoot, like fireworks, out from a bowl, held in place by a hidden pin holder.
right The narrow confines of a metal container allow a sheaf of daffodils to stride across on the diagonal without toppling.
opposite page Several gerberas float lazily at the centre of a shallow glass bowl.

opaque, in a geometric or otherwise unfussy shape, will not only complement the furnishings in contemporary interiors, but it will also give precedence to the flowers, giving them free rein to proclaim their beauty without competition. The red gerbera daisies pictured opposite, floating in a wide, shallow bowl on a table, make an understated and sophisticated design statement, whereas an oversized, elaborate centrepiece studded with blossoms would look too stiff and conventional. In settings such as this monastic, modern dining room, restraint is always the best way to go. As architect Mies van der Rohe proclaimed, less is more, and in simple modern rooms let it be so.

opposite page and left
Binding or encasing stems of flowers that demonstrate a tendency to droop not only maintains their rigidity, but also creates a display with more contemporary flair than if they splayed out every which way. Here, several bunches of paper-white narcissi are bundled like a sheaf of wheat with loops of heavy-gauge galvanized steel wire. The handcrafted porcelain vase holding the perfumed bouquet looks as if it has been torn and sculpted from paper dipped in plaster. The serrated rim echoes the fringe of petals. *below right* A curvaceous, orange-tinged vase proves an ideal cohort for a ruffled topknot of tightly packed, like-hued parrot tulips.

bold & sculptural

When arranging flowers, many people consider only the sensuous impact the actual blossoms will have on the beholder. But flowers are more than just blossoms – they are also composed of stems, leaves and roots. And then there are the myriad other forms a flowering plant may assume, such as a tree, shrub or vine. Taking an artistic risk with an arrangement rather than sticking to the tried and tested, may therefore result from an impulse to experiment with the delightful and novel shapes and textures of tall, smooth stems, glossy leaves, rustling grasses, bare branches and sculptural seedpods.

Succumbing to the allure of a rustling armful of grasses, the drama
of a naked bough or the curves of an intricately patterned seedpod is,
for some people, a daring and unconventional flight of fancy. To others,
foliage, twigs and seedpods are every bit as pleasing to the eye as
a lavish posy of roses and, moreover, they serve as an intriguing
reminder of the wealth of different forms in the plant kingdom.

Working with sculptural plant matter requires a bold hand and eye.
Such items usually are at their best with spare, contemporary rooms as
a backdrop. By their very nature, after all, bold and sculptural displays
are intended to stand out, to demand attention from onlookers. Scale is
important. An armful of bare branches may look magnificent, but make

Exhibiting a few select
leaves or blooms creates
the impression of haiku.
left In a lustrous black bowl,
a pair of puckered ligularia
leaves arch over a collection of
river-smoothed black pebbles
centred by a silvery stone.
right Like birds in flight,
several calla lilies wheel
around each other inside
a glass goldfish bowl. When
working with callas, it pays to
remember that they exude a
slimy sap that can hasten their
decay; to eliminate this, sit
them in a separate bucket of
tepid water for a couple of
hours to 'bleed' the sap before
arranging them in your bowl.

everyday arrangements

Shoots and branches are best appreciated when arrayed in minimalist, unfussy containers that whisper rather than shout. *opposite page* Furry, pearl-grey catkins are one of spring's earliest signs that warmth – and colour – are soon to surface from the monochrome shadings of winter. Indeed, all it takes is a few branches of pussy willow to herald the onset of nature's new year. *left* A handful of willowy grasses leans gracefully over the rim of a translucent vase. *right* Similarly, narrow bamboo shoots are sliced to different lengths to offset a pair of fraternal vases, whose gentle colours imply that they are stand-ins for actual blooms.

sure they don't impede your progress into a room, or threaten to catch your hair or poke you in the eye. Dramatic arrangements require some space around them, and thus are better kept for spacious rooms. In contrast, if twigs, pods or vines are delicate, they need to be displayed where they can be studied – and admired – close up.

Idiosyncratic plant matter appears most striking when breathing space is given to the individual elements, such as nodes, pods, leaf forms or feathery foliage. The choice of container is important, too, for it should be able to hold its own and synchronize with what it embraces, or else the display will appear top-heavy and out of place, no matter where you set it down, be it on a sill, shelf, table or floor.

bold & sculptural

this page and inset, below
Tall, loose-limbed sprays of
cherry perform a star turn in an
otherwise empty hallway. When
pruning branches in the wild,
choose ones that bear firm,
plump buds. Once indoors, slit
the bottoms of the branches with
a sharp knife to expose pith to
water so branches and blossoms
can receive enough to drink.

wild at heart

Due to the rise of globalization and
e-commerce, virtually any and every
exotic or unusual flower you can think
of is now available at any time or in any
place, through florists or at the click of
a mouse. Despite this, seasonal blooms
and our indigenous wild flowers still seem
to exert a powerful appeal. Perhaps this
is because – through the plants, grasses
and trees that are familiar to us – we feel
more rooted to the earth and more
connected to Mother Nature.

These arrangements are a far cry from
the conventional 'flower arrangement'.
Bare branches, or those studded with
emerging blossom, introduce a breath
of fresh air into an interior. Dried leaves,
seedpods and clusters of jewel-like

this page and inset, right Branches need not have blossoms to hold visual appeal. Even bare branches can be showstoppers, when presented in a container that catches the eye.

wild at heart

this page and opposite page
An elegant, Japanese-style arrangement of cherry blossoms is composed of two sprays lopped from a flowering tree. Floral tape holds the branches in position against one side of the comb-textured earthenware vase. Part of the enchantment of viewing this display is wondering how the vase maintains its balance, a feeling intensified by the fact that it's deliberately placed off-centre on the table.

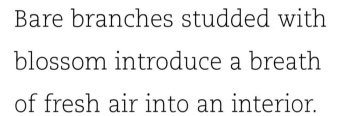

Bare branches studded with blossom introduce a breath of fresh air into an interior.

berries are like treasure trove, brought inside and put on display, inviting onlookers to marvel over them and admire their fine detailing, examining the network of veins on a leaf, the intricate structure of a seedpod or the lustrous glow of autumn berries.

Each season holds its own particular delights. In the spring, flowering shrubs and trees abound in the garden, and pruning them of a few branches will only enhance future growth. Summer grasses are long and luxuriant. At the beach, there's driftwood to collect. And at this time of year, when flowers and plants are at their most abundant and plentiful,

some specimens can be dried, including roses and lavender, and herbs such as yarrow, allowing us to enjoy them for weeks instead of just a few days. Some plant matter will last indefinitely. During the autumn, falling leaves can be collected and preserved to add to a floral display or to showcase alone, either pressed flat in frames or standing in a container. In darkest winter, arrangements of dried leaves and branches will remind you of the spring that is to come. Alternatively, glossy evergreens and bright berries practically beg to be clipped and displayed throughout the house, or even used to adorn the Christmas dinner table.

above left A trio of containers display an armful of blossom in the light shining through a leaded window into an upper hallway. Placing plants and flowers on the floor rather than on a table causes them to be appreciated for their sculptural qualities, rather than just as an assembly of blooms.

above right When preserved, autumn leaves can be collected in a container, where they will keep for weeks. One way to preserve leaves is to iron them; another is to press them between pieces of tissue or paper that are weighted with a heavy book, until the leaves are flat and dry.

everyday arrangements

This page Coiled ivies and rosy-cheeked pears occupy a cylindrical vase in the manner of an aquarium; the vase alongside showcases hypericum berries.
inset, above Collected in a pottery vase, blackberries look as succulent as if they were still on the vine.

The shape of a bouquet is a sure sign that it has been conceived and created with romance in mind.

left A tender-hearted nosegay mimics a bridal bouquet, especially when it is arranged and displayed in a vase associated with celebration, such as a sterling-silver cup.

inset, below Another loving gesture is to snip dainty little sprigs of a favourite flower, such as sweet peas, and gather them together in a group of mismatched vases.

right and below Sweet peas live up to their dulcet nomenclature, composed as they are of fragile petals and graceful tendrils unfurling from vinelike stems. They impart a lovely scent as well. Colours are painterly, ranging from blush and lavender to shades of violet and red. In the vase, sweet peas do not last as long as some of their more robust cohorts. Even so, nothing is more alluring than a bouquet of these enchanting blooms. Here, lavender-pink sweet peas peep over the rim of a bottle tinted pale chartreuse.

romantic & relaxed

It has been said that home is an extension of the self, and that each room expresses a different dimension or aspect of that self. Some rooms, like sitting or dining rooms, turn a formal face to the world; others, like the kitchen, seem more welcoming and friendly. Intimate rooms, such as the bedroom and bathroom, succour our secret selves. In our private quarters, we are at our most vulnerable and exposed. Different flowers are suited to these different areas, and softer, more spontaneous arrangements are particularly suited to our private spaces, where we yield to our most uninhibited and passionate desires.

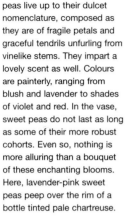

When creating arrangements for bedrooms, bathrooms and boudoirs, bear in mind that the aim is to create a little oasis of calm, whatever the surroundings may be. All the arrangements shown on these pages invite the observer to pause and spend a few minutes engaged in quiet contemplation. Of course, many of them would work just as well in halls and sitting rooms, where their tranquil good looks and often feminine charms are guaranteed to seduce any visitors.

opposite page, main picture and inset Although they bloom a short time – only a couple of weeks, in fact – lily of the valley proves utterly irresistible, not only in the garden, but indoors as well, where its delicate bell-like blooms release a powerful perfume. Is it no wonder, then, that they are a sublime accompaniment to dreams?

This page Sometimes flowers just beg to be picked or purchased, even when a conventional container is nowhere at hand. More humble objects can also be pressed into service, like this food tin, which was sprayed with quick-drying white paint. Voilà! A container that stands up and sings. A ribbon adds a final decorative flourish.

More than any other attribute, the key to the mood a flower inspires is its colour. Dramatic, eye-catching blooms tend to make their presence felt through their rich or vibrant colours. Think of acid-green chrysanthemums or pillar-box red amaryllis. Other, more modest flowers are more reserved and allusive, tending towards subtler, romantic tints rather than bold saturated hues. Dramatic flowers often display a bold, sculptural profile and unusual textures, too. In contrast, their softer, more demure cousins, such as sweet peas, roses, lilac, poppies and anemones, bear abundant delicate petals with a fragile, silky texture. If you want to create romantic effects, choose plants that stand out by virtue of their

left and opposite page A gracious assembly of shapely clear-glass bottles runs the gamut from collector's item to everyday-ordinary. All unite in democratic harmony when ranked in rows to display an mix of wild flowers and cutting-garden blooms. By giving each particular species of flower its own individual bottle, the display achieves the same patrician aura as meticulously documented specimens rendered in botanical prints by such celebrated masters of the genre as Redouté.

romantic & relaxed

delicacy or exquisite flower formations. If these flowers are sweetly scented, such as, for example, lily of the valley, sweet peas or dwarf narcissi, their charms will only be heightened. Scented flowers are particularly delicious in the bedroom, where they can be appreciated first thing in the morning and last thing at night.

Our reaction to a vase of flowers is also affected by the manner in which they are displayed. A single flower, or a cluster of one type of flowers, of virtually any variety, looks more bold and modern and makes a stronger design statement than, say, a loose armful of mixed blooms in a terracotta jug, which will appear more informal and uncontrived. Unconventional arrangements, such as flowers floating in a shallow bowl, or wrapped inside a glass vase, also create more funky, cutting-edge effects. For more private and

To see or not to see... Do you want to focus attention on the flower or the container? *right and opposite page* When the flower is as tantalizing and unusual as these tassels of love-lies-bleeding, the answer seems obvious: let the eye delight in the graceful blooms and their velvety companions, long-stemmed roses. When flowers are as arresting as these, the bottles require no provenance at all. Indeed, the troop that marches across this mantelpiece includes the most eclectic of containers: an old porcelain-capped ginger-beer bottle, a milk bottle and, alongside, another that once dispensed olive oil.

For romantic effects, choose plants that stand out by virtue of their exquisite flower formations.

Romantic arrangements often combine a seemingly random combination of blooms in a manner that belies the thought behind their selection.
left A loose bunch of wild flowers and shrub roses.
below left Pink-tinged ranunculus peep over a cluster of pink peppercorns.
opposite page Flowers do not necessarily look their best in formal displays – a point that's proven by a bucket of paper whites and a simple jug of delphiniums.

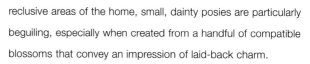

reclusive areas of the home, small, dainty posies are particularly beguiling, especially when created from a handful of compatible blossoms that convey an impression of laid-back charm.

The container that holds your arrangement should be similar in spirit to the flowers it houses. For soft, romantic effects, almost anything can be pressed into service – a vintage perfume bottle, a fragile antique teacup, a rustic jug or a ceramic vase shaped and signed by a potter's hand – the more eclectic, the better. These individual, one-off containers create small arrangements that have the exquisite air of a still-life. Even a humble tin spray-painted for the occasion will help communicate a bouquet's – or single blossom's – sweet nostalgic charm. And the time it takes (even if only five minutes) to match up blooms and vase is time well spent, for it is spent entirely on ourselves, making these flowers the most meaningful flowers of all.

Because they articulate heartfelt sentiments, certain days of the year – such as Valentine's Day and Mother's Day – have become synonymous with floral gifts. But any day or occasion can be made special with flowers: the birth of a new baby, perhaps, or an informal drinks party for friends. Any time you feel the need to celebrate!

Often it's the simplest touches that elevate gesture to gift. *opposite page* When already arranged in a handsome glass vase, accented with seedpods and a 'handle' fashioned from Virginia creeper, these mophead hydrangeas make the perfect gift for a busy hostess. *left* The juxtaposition of homespun hessian and an eye-catching 'diamond' brooch is certain to elicit a chorus of admiring 'oohs' and 'aahs'. *below right* A handful of fresh-faced pansies requires no further adornment than a ribbon tie. What lends this little posy its singular appeal is the texture of the ribbon – lush velvet, to match the petals.

wrapped bunches

The very words 'special occasion' often elicit a sensation of complete paralysis. Uttered in a supercilious tone, the phrase conjures up visions of media-blitz photo opportunities – a society wedding, perhaps, or a formal dinner party that would put royalty to shame. But this need not be the case. Special occasions are just that: occasions made special in ways that surprise and delight. And what better way to celebrate such an occasion than with a bunch of flowers? Additional touches, such as a dainty adornment or length of ribbon, will turn your floral offering into a special gesture.

valentine's day

Since time immemorial, flowers have been equated with romance, especially on Valentine's Day, a day consecrated to lovers, which harks back to Roman times, when the date was dedicated to 'love lotteries'. Names of young virgins were rolled into balls, placed in a bowl, and selected at random by Roman soldiers seeking brides. A similar tale dates to the Middle Ages: on 14 February, it is said, birds paired off, and young men, after drawing names from a bowl, wore their 'hearts' on their sleeves for a week, hoping for a positive response from their potential mates.

Today's pairings are happily not confined to lotteries. Instead, Valentine's Day is marked by cards, chocolates and flowers. Indeed, it is estimated that 100 million Valentine's flowers are sent or given each year as tokens of affection. Most are long-stemmed red roses, which signify beauty, love and passion.

this page and inset, left
Who's to say that roses are a strictly male purview? Flout convention and surprise the man in your life with not one, but three dozen, roses, wrapped up in his favourite newspaper and secured with a hank of black raffia.

opposite page, above and below The Victorians adored posies, especially ones containing violas, which carry the message, 'I return your love.' Slip some pots into a pretty heart-shaped box, or present a bunch on top of a box of chocolates instead.

When Cupid strikes, grab a bouquet and enjoy the ride!

Fragile, fragrant flowers in delicious hues
express the joy and wonder of a new birth.

new baby

Of all the special occasions that stand out in a busy and eventful life, none is more special, perhaps, than the birth of a child. And nothing proclaims the arrival of a newborn more joyfully than a gift of flowers. Indeed, many flowers resemble children in their open-faced purity, especially those sweet-natured ones with clusters of delicate, scented petals. Arrangements needn't be complicated or time-consuming. A posy of specially chosen flowers, put together with thought and care, is far more meaningful than a huge cellophane-clad bouquet ordered over the phone.

These quick and easy posies are a wonderful way to welcome a child into the world, and to honour the parents as well. *opposite page* Simple, fragrant paper whites give the impression of being freshly plucked from a bountiful meadow.
above A newborn baby girl is the lucky recipient of a sunny nosegay of spray roses, grouped in a vintage teacup that will be hers for life. Because it contains buds and partial blooms as well as open ones, the arrangement should last at least a week.
right Queen Anne's lace haloes a dainty cluster of white roses.

There are many approaches to making a Mother's Day gift of flowers truly memorable. One is to select a vase or container that is, in its own way, guaranteed to please your mum.
opposite page Ranunculus in a minimalist white bowl exuberantly mimic the effect of an explosion of happy thoughts.
left A single poppy anemone adds a flamboyant flourish to lasting tokens of love: an antique demitasse, a string of pearls and a silver locket.
below Delight mum with morning tea in bed – and an antique vase of red and white dahlias accented with the floral fireworks of soon-to-bloom buds.

mother's day

Where would we be without mothers? Our mums nurture us throughout our lives, both physically and emotionally. They administer to us when we are ill, listen with empathy (and patience) to complaints both real and imagined, and glory in all our triumphs and successes, no matter how small. In other words, they are no less than saints!

Religions both ancient and modern pay tribute to their own deities but, in terms of lifelong devotion and concern for our wellbeing, no saint in the world can measure up to one's very own, one-of-a-kind mum. Indeed, even though mothers are recognized and honoured on a day set aside for them, one could argue that we need at least a week to

Soft pastels such as blush and lavender have a feminine feel that is perfectly suited to Mother's Day flowers, while brighter hues – see the zingy ranunculus on page 51 – convey feelings of enthusiasm and zest.

This page A simple bouquet of peonies and viburnum caps a crystal vase. Bouquets like these are quick and easy to create. Start with the central flower, then criss-cross stems while turning the bouquet, making sure blossoms barely 'kiss' each other. Once the bouquet achieves the desired fullness, secure stems with floral tape and cut them straight across for a tidy look.

opposite page The twin trumpets of a 1950s-era vase showcase porcelain-like roses, cornflowers and catmint.

celebrate them properly! Like many special occasions, Mother's Day is often commemorated with a family meal, as well as by cards and gifts of plants and flowers. Floral tributes need not be extravagant or elaborate. It's the carefully thought-out presentation that sets the flowers shown here apart. Choose your mum's favourite blooms, then think about how best to dress them up for her.

Because Mother's Day falls in spring, the choice of flowers is profuse. This is the season of tree- and shrub-born blossoms, such as apple, cherry and lilac, which can be offered and displayed on their own, or in tandem with other compatible blooms. Spring is the time, too, when the most heavenly perfumed flowers come into bloom, which enhances the experience of giving, and receiving, a Mother's Day bouquet.

A beautiful vase enhances a bouquet, and it may even become an heirloom to treasure always.

Simple is best when it comes to summer entertaining – tables often look their most inviting when they are dressed in an informal manner.

below A single sprig of fragrant lavender is tucked into a ribbon-tied napkin, creating a simple, rustic effect.

right If you have only seconds to spare, slip single roses into simple glass vases. Put one at each place, or pop them at one end of the table, where these perfect specimens can be admired without their getting in the way.

opposite page Individual place settings have been personalized by folding napkins around small pots of tiny blue flowers. Each napkin is tied in place with snappy red-and-white cord. You could substitute raffia, ribbon or brightly coloured shoelaces.

relaxed summer meals

In a way, summer itself is a special occasion because it's puncuated by lots of mini-celebrations – picnics in the park, barbecues and long, lingering meals with family and friends. Summer's the season, too, for indulging in all that's fresh: fresh air, fresh produce and, of course, fresh flowers, which are at their most abundant at this time of year. If it's hot, no one wants to go to too much trouble to create an elaborate table setting. Five minutes is about the maximum length of time most of us are willing to dedicate to setting the table and throwing together some flowers that will enhance the effect we're after. To simplify the process, keep a collection of pretty containers at hand, and a pair of scissors, and you're sure to be ready for anything!

Surprise your guests with an unexpected twist on a presumed floral arrangement. *this page* Instead of being stood upright in a standard display of multiple blooms, a voluptuous frilled peony and a full-blown tea rose unfurl and float – like dainty aquatic denizens of the deep – in a bubble-shaped fish bowl. For balance, water fills the bowl to just below the halfway mark, which allows the blossoms plenty of room to breathe. *opposite page* More peonies, minus their stems, wreathe the bowl, and mingle in elegant disarray with dendrobium orchid heads and rose petals.

left Rose and orchid heads are showcased in wine and water glasses at each place setting. A scattering of rose petals and dendrobium heads accents each plate. When guests remove the glasses, they can cluster them around the centrepiece to create a veritable garden.

dining in the pink

Most festive occasions centre round a meal. And, be it intimate or grand, nothing establishes the tone of that meal more effectively than the table setting. Here, a summery, romantic scheme takes as its basis every shade of pink, from creamy, blush-tinged roses to candy-floss-coloured peonies and fuchsia dendrobium orchids. The overall effect is one of lush extravagance, but it has been achieved with only three or four stems of each type of flower. The large goldfish bowl makes a dramatic centrepiece, but this spectacular effect takes only minutes to create, while the flower heads in glasses at each place setting are similarly swift to put together.

impromptu
celebrations

Sometimes the most memorable celebrations are those that require no planning at all. Inviting a few friends in for drinks after work or at the weekend, for example, can be as spontaneous as a sigh of relief at the end of a hectic week. All you need are a few bottles of wine and some tempting nibbles.

What makes the magic? The white tablecloth signals a special occasion – an effect heightened by the delicate glasses and the deliciously pretty flowers. This visual feast may only take a few minutes to create, but it's equally suitable for a Mother's Day lunch, hen party or baby shower. For a last-minute gathering, blooms may only be partially opened; standing them in warm water will encourage them to unfurl slightly.

Potted plants and cut flowers provide instant ambience at a last-minute get-together.

opposite page, below Clustering plants in one spot establishes a colourful backdrop for the table.

opposite page, above Blossoms clipped to the correct stem length are tucked into glasses to be interspersed with the food and drink.

this page A bowl of limes can be treated as decoration, too, especially when blooms and petals are swiftly scattered among the fruit.

inset, above A single blossom placed on each plate adds to the festive atmosphere.

When 'less is more', the eye finds itself drawn to the discriminating choice of objects.

They look a million dollars, but these minimalist settings take moments to put together.
this page Green anthuriums and grasses stand in etched glass vases; more grasses are knotted around the napkins.
inset, above The leaflike anthuriums stand out by virtue of their heart shape, quilted texture and glossy shine.
opposite page A dramatic orchid blossom welcomes each guest to a table set for a Sunday brunch with friends.
opposite page, inset Place cards are simple tags tied to each bloom.

minimalist magic

Many people equate celebration with the opportunity to pull out all the stops in terms of decoration; others, by contrast, are masters of the minimal, relying on a few carefully selected objects to make a statement.

In this scenario, the tabletop is transformed into an avant-garde stage for a meticulous presentation of food and drink. A monochromatic palette provides a clean backdrop for the bold, understated floral flourishes, which rely on unconventional flowers and foliage to create visual impact. Colour – metaphorically speaking – arises out of the food and conversation, which is precisely what makes a meal special!

sources

VASES AND CONTAINERS

Artisan Home
www.artisanhome.com
Striking contemporary glass and
ceramic vases as well as unusual
handmade pottery vases and bowls.

The Conran Shop
Michelin House
81 Fulham Road
London SW3 6RD
020 7589 7401
www.conran.co.uk
Cutting-edge designs, including clear
glass vases in a multitude of different
shapes and sizes.

Designer's Guild
267 Kings Road
London SW3 5EN
020 7351 5775
www.designersguild.com
Decorative vases, pottery and
tableware, including architectural
vases designed by Christian Tortu.

Dibor
Visit www.dibor.co.uk or call 0870
0133 666 for a mail-order catalogue.
Antique-style French-inspired
ceramics, glassware and glass vases
in relaxed rustic styles.

Habitat
196 Tottenham Court Road
London W1T 7LG
Call 0845 601 0740 or visit
www.habitat.net for details of your
nearest store.
Wide range of metal, wooden and
glass vases. Also sells galvanized
metal florist's buckets.

Heal's
196 Tottenham Court Road
London W1T 7LQ
020 7636 1666
www.heals.co.uk
Cool and classic vases in glass and
ceramics. Also baskets and
decorative kitchenware.

India Jane
131–133 King's Road
London SW3 4PW
020 73511060
Antique-style ceramic vases, bowls
and planters. Also glass vases,
decorative bottles, storm lamps and
mercury glassware.

John Lewis
Oxford Street
London W1A 1EX
020 7629 7711
Visit www.johnlewis.com for details
of your nearest store.
A good range of affordable vases,
glassware and other containers.

LSA International
Call 01932 789721 or visit www.lsa-
international.co.uk for details of your
nearest stockist.
Contemporary homewares brand
that includes stylish glass and
porcelain vases. Stocked by a wide
variety of retailers, from department
stores to boutiques.

Mint
70 Wigmore Street
London W1U 2SQ
020 7224 4406
Rubber vases and other quirky,
idiosyncratic designs.

Models Own
2 Fairfax Place
Dartmouth
Devon TQ6 9AD
0800 169 9228
www.modelsown.com
Modern, retro- and country-style
vases.

OKA
Visit www.okadirect.com or call 0870
160 6002 for a mail-order catalogue
or details of their stores.
Chic accessories, including faux
bamboo vases, rattan pots, ceramic
vases and decorative planters.

Purves and Purves
220–224 Tottenham Court Road
London W1T 7QE
020 7580 8223
www.purves.co.uk
Funky vases, including the Alessi
collection and other plastic vases.

Selfridges
400 Oxford Street
London W1A 1AB
020 7629 1234
and at:
1 The Dome
The Trafford Centre
Manchester M17 8DA
0161 629 1234
www.selfridges.co.uk
Designer accessories from around
the world.

Skandium
86 Marylebone High Street
London W1U 4QS
020 7935 2077
www.skandium.com
Modern Scandinavian designs.

Vessel
114 Kensington Park Road
London W11 2PW
020 7727 8001
Contemporary glass and ceramics,
from iconic Scandinavian design to
flamboyant Italian art glass.

Woolworths
Visit www.woolworths.co.uk or call
0845 608 1101 for details of your
nearest store.
Small range of stylish vases, baskets
and other containers, at low prices.

FLOWER MARKETS

Columbia Road Flower Market
Columbia Road
London E2 7QB
Sundays 08.00–14.00

Covent Garden Market
Nine Elms
London SW8 5NX
www.cgma.gov.uk/flowers.htm

Flower Market
Market Precinct
Pershore Street
Birmingham B5 6UW
0121 622 4111
Flower Market

Bernard Street
Southampton SO14 2NS
023 8022 1212

New Smithfield Market
Whitworth Street East
Openshaw
Manchester M11 2WJ
0161 223 9036/9639

Yorkshire Produce Centre
Pontefract Lane
Leeds LS9 0PS
0113 201 9888

FLOWERS ONLINE

Sunflowers Direct
www.sunflowersdirect.co.uk
Fresh cut flowers delivered boxed,
with long stems ready to be cut
down and arranged.

David Austin Roses
www.davidaustinroses.com
Exquisite, cut-flower fragrant English
roses in delicious colours. Easy to
arrange alone or with other flowers.

To find retail florists in your area, visit
the Flowers and Plants Association
website at www.flowers.org

picture credits